Inside Animals

Reptiles

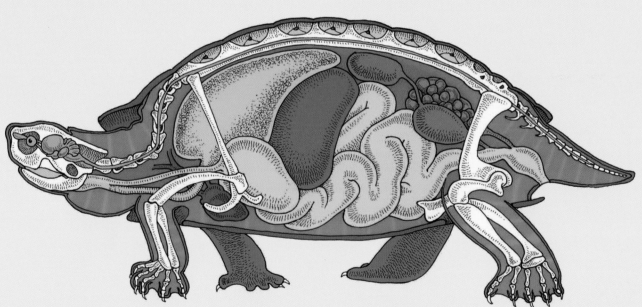

David West

WAYLAND

Wayland
First published in Great Britain in 2018 by Hodder and Stoughton

Designed and illustrated by David West

HB ISBN 978 1 5263 1069 9
PB ISBN 978 1 5263 1070 5

Printed in Malaysia

Wayland
An imprint of
Hachette Children's Group
Carmelite House
50 Victoria Embankment
London EC4Y 0DZ

An Hachette UK Company
www.hachette.co.uk

www.wayland.co.uk

INSIDE ANIMALS REPTILES
was produced for Wayland by
David West Children's Books, 11 Glebe Road, London SW13 0DR

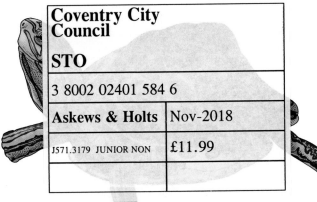

FSC
www.fsc.org

MIX
Paper from
responsible sources
FSC® C010875

Contents

Lizard   4

Inside a Lizard   6

Chameleon   8

Inside a Chameleon   10

Crocodile   12

Inside a Crocodile   14

Turtle   16

Inside a Turtle   18

Snake   20

Inside a Snake   22

Glossary and Index   24

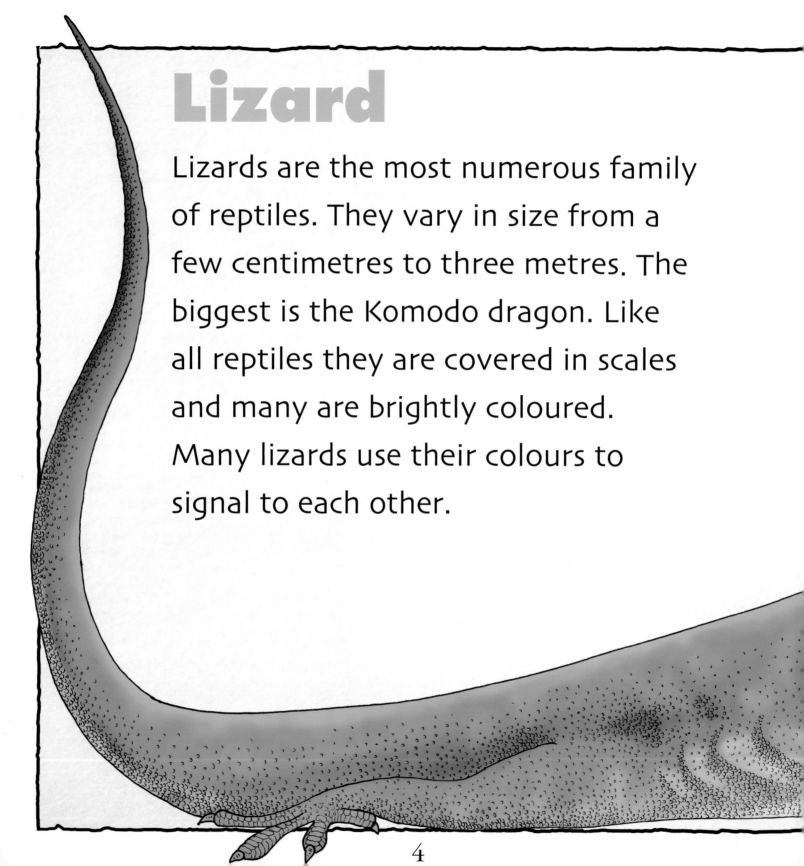

Lizard

Lizards are the most numerous family of reptiles. They vary in size from a few centimetres to three metres. The biggest is the Komodo dragon. Like all reptiles they are covered in scales and many are brightly coloured. Many lizards use their colours to signal to each other.

This anole lizard uses its brightly-coloured throat pouch, called a dewlap, to signal to other anole lizards. The throat patch is hidden when not signalling because the bright colours would be seen by **predators**.

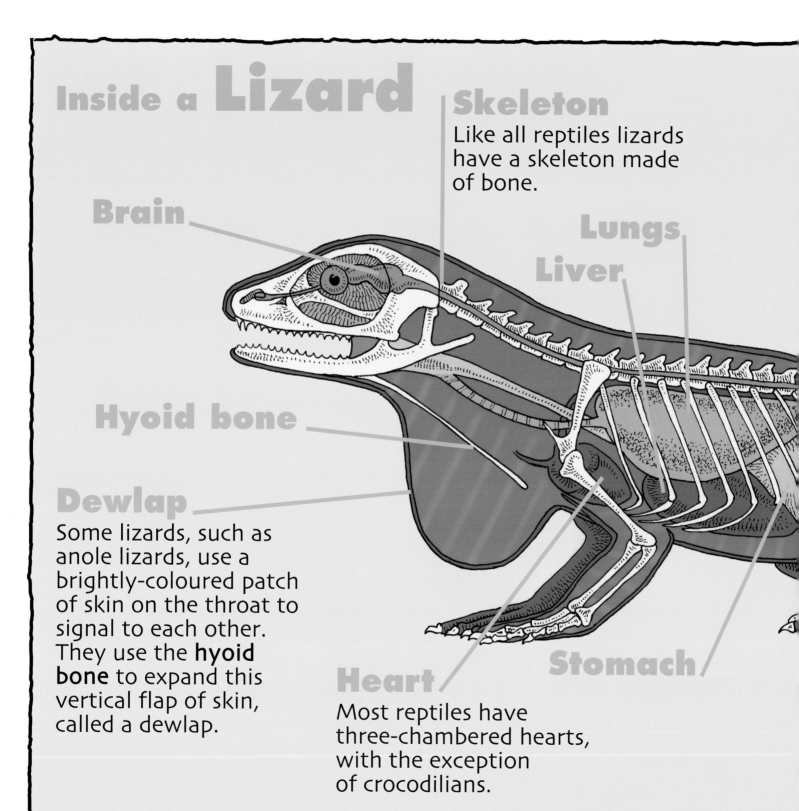

Inside a Lizard

Skeleton
Like all reptiles lizards have a skeleton made of bone.

Brain

Lungs

Liver

Hyoid bone

Dewlap
Some lizards, such as anole lizards, use a brightly-coloured patch of skin on the throat to signal to each other. They use the **hyoid bone** to expand this vertical flap of skin, called a dewlap.

Heart
Most reptiles have three-chambered hearts, with the exception of crocodilians.

Stomach

Ovaries

Most lizards lay eggs. Some give birth to live young after eggs have developed inside the mother.

Tail

Many lizards can shed their tail to escape predators. A lizard's tail can grow back in a few weeks.

Kidneys

Bladder

Digestion

Lizards digest their chewed food of insects in their stomach and intestines.

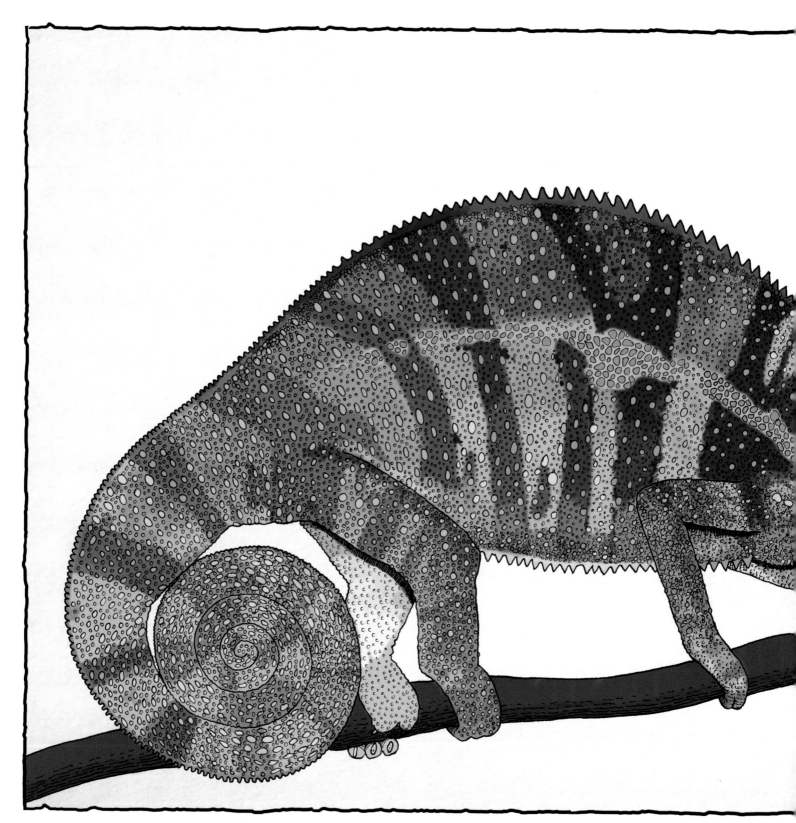

Chameleon

Chameleons are lizards that can change colour to blend into the background. They are excellent climbers. They have special feet that grip branches and their tails can grip too. Their two eyes can look in different directions to spot predators or **prey**. They feed mainly on insects, catching them with their long, sticky tongues.

As well as to camouflage themselves, chameleons change colour to signal to each other. Temperature also affects their colouring.

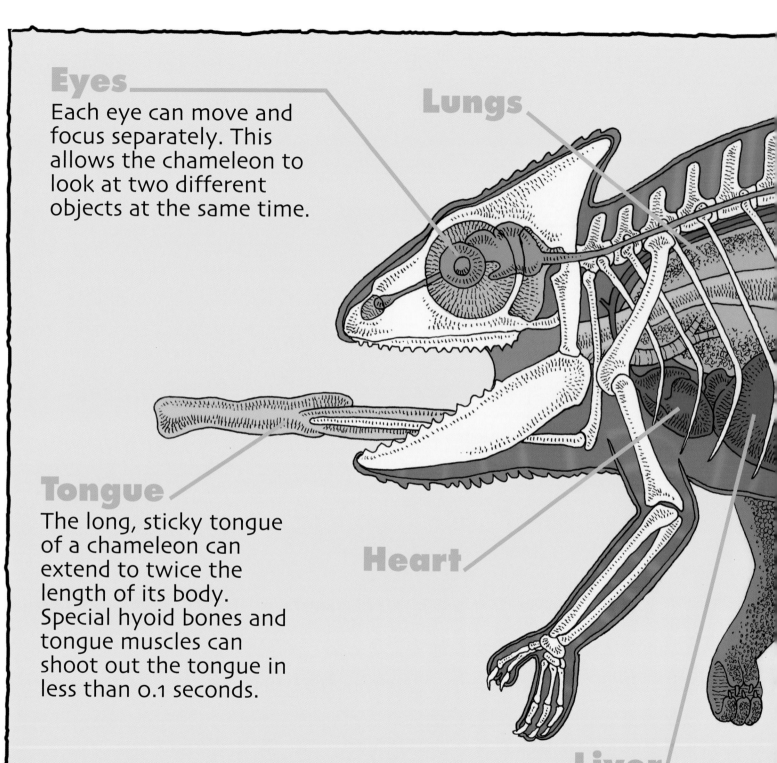

Eyes

Each eye can move and focus separately. This allows the chameleon to look at two different objects at the same time.

Lungs

Tongue

The long, sticky tongue of a chameleon can extend to twice the length of its body. Special hyoid bones and tongue muscles can shoot out the tongue in less than 0.1 seconds.

Heart

Liver

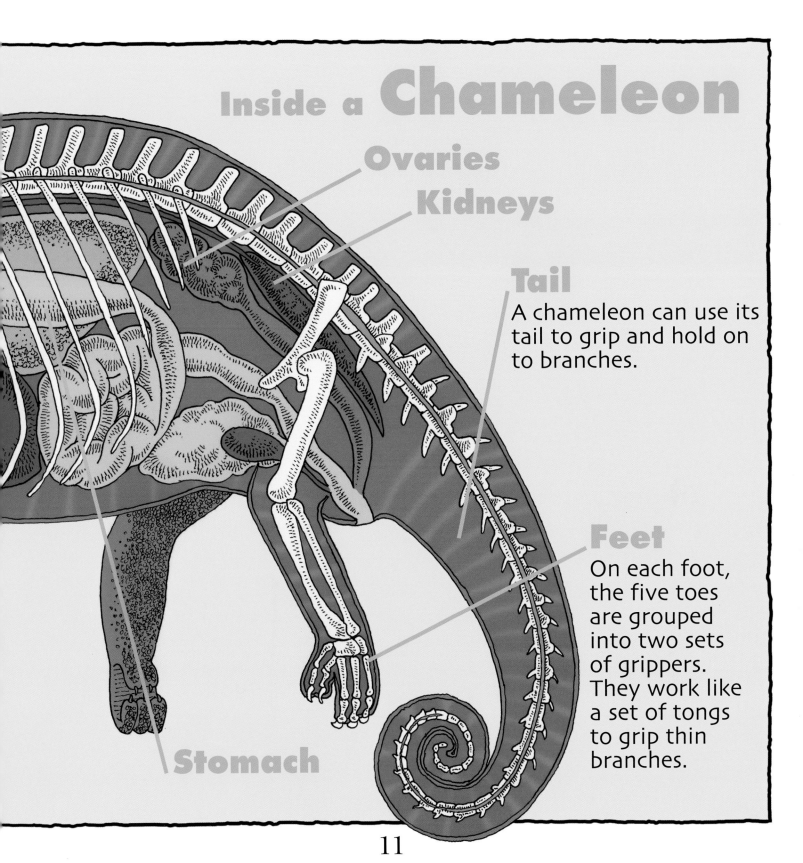

Inside a **Chameleon**

Ovaries

Kidneys

Tail

A chameleon can use its tail to grip and hold on to branches.

Feet

On each foot, the five toes are grouped into two sets of grippers. They work like a set of tongs to grip thin branches.

Stomach

Crocodile

Crocodiles are the largest members of the reptile family. They live in swamps, rivers and some saltwater environments around the world. They have been around since the age of the dinosaurs and have changed very little since then. They are aggressive hunters and feed on fish, reptiles, **amphibians**, **crustaceans**, **molluscs**, birds and mammals as large as elephants.

Crocodiles are ambush predators. They wait, concealed underwater, and rush out to grab their prey with surprising speed. Their powerful jaws grip their prey and drag it under the water to drown it.

Inside a Crocodile

Armoured plates
Underneath the outer layer of skin are bony plates called osteoderms. These provide further armour.

Armoured skin
The outer layer of the thick skin has armoured scales which protect it from predators.

Tail muscles
Powerful muscles swing the tail from side to side to power the crocodile through the water.

Skeleton
The skeleton of crocodiles has barely changed over the last 200 million years.

Lungs

Crocodiles breathe air but they can hold their breath underwater for more than an hour.

Nose

Its nose holes and eyes are high on its head. This means it can still breathe and see while most of its body lies underwater out of sight.

Brain

Kidney

Throat

Crocodiles have flaps in their throat so they can eat while submerged without also swallowing water.

Liver

Heart

Crocodiles have a flap in their heart that sends extra blood to the stomach to help digest food.

Stomach

The stomach has pebbles in it that help grind up unchewed food.

Turtle

Turtles are reptiles with a special bony shell that protects them from predators. Most turtles can pull their heads into their shell. They all live in water except for tortoises which live only on land. There are many types that live their entire lives at sea. They breathe air and lay leathery eggs on land.

*Some turtles, like this terrapin, live in fresh or **brackish** water. They feed on plants and small animals such as insects, snails and worms.*

Inside a **Turtle**

Lungs
Turtles have lungs and must surface to breathe air.

Skeleton
The turtle skeleton is divided into two, the endoskeleton and the exoskeleton. The internal bones make up the endoskeleton and the exoskeleton is its shell.

Brain

Head
Some turtles can withdraw their head into the shell for protection.

Heart

Stomach

Liver
This is the largest organ and helps with digestion.

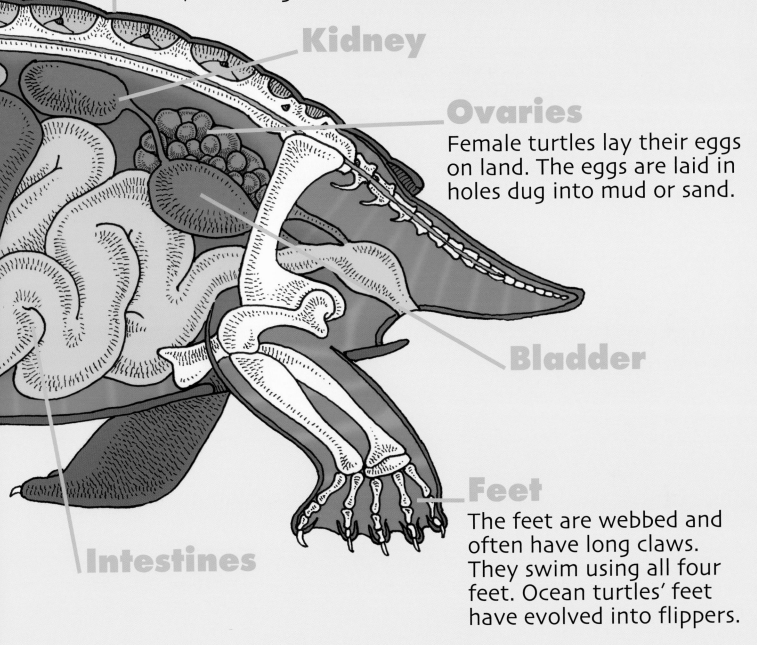

Shell

The outer layer is covered with bony scales made of **keratin**. The inner layer of the shell is made of bones, including the backbone and the ribs.

Kidney

Ovaries

Female turtles lay their eggs on land. The eggs are laid in holes dug into mud or sand.

Bladder

Feet

The feet are webbed and often have long claws. They swim using all four feet. Ocean turtles' feet have evolved into flippers.

Intestines

Snake

Snakes are legless reptiles. Although most live on land, some can be found in the sea. They are cold-blooded like lizards, which means they cannot generate their own body heat. Unlike lizards they do not have eyelids. Some snakes use poison to kill their prey. They have sharp fangs to inject the poison into the prey. Snakes swallow their prey whole. They have elastic jaws so they can swallow animals bigger than their heads.

This cobra expands its rib bones to create a hood that warns predators away. It can also squirt venom from its fangs which can blind its attacker.

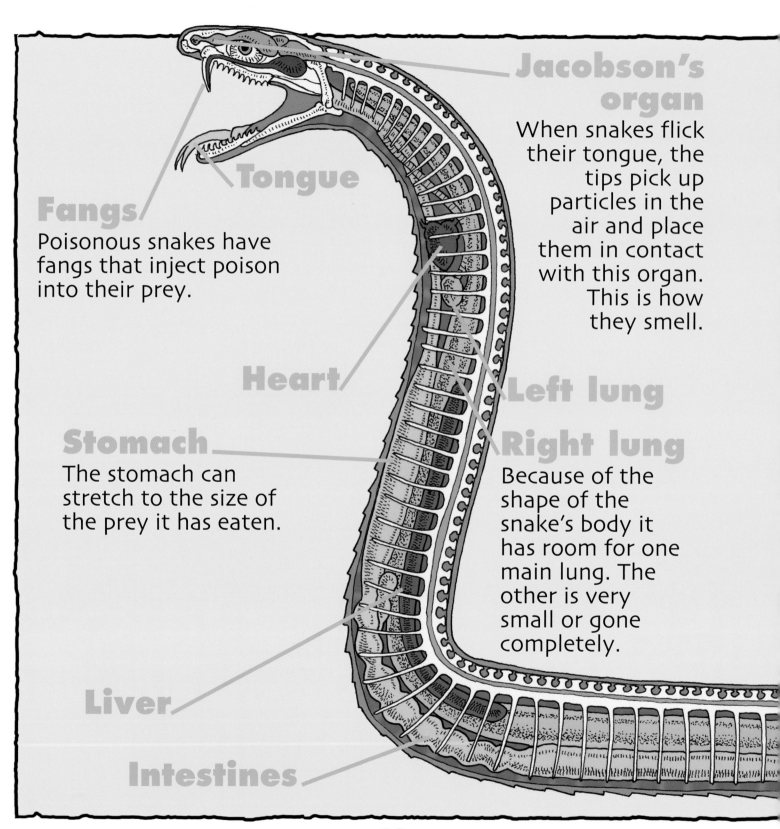

Jacobson's organ

When snakes flick their tongue, the tips pick up particles in the air and place them in contact with this organ. This is how they smell.

Tongue

Fangs

Poisonous snakes have fangs that inject poison into their prey.

Heart

Left lung

Right lung

Because of the shape of the snake's body it has room for one main lung. The other is very small or gone completely.

Stomach

The stomach can stretch to the size of the prey it has eaten.

Liver

Intestines

Inside a **Snake**

Skin
Like all reptiles' skin the snake's skin is made up of scales. As the snake grows, its skin is shed at certain times. This shedding is called moulting.

Skeleton
Snakes can have between 200 and 400 vertebrae in their backbone.

Ovaries
Most species of snakes lay eggs. The eggs are leathery like most reptiles' eggs.

Kidneys

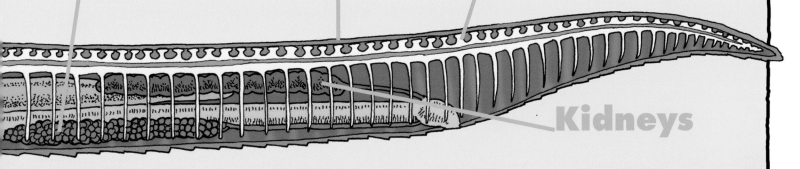

Glossary

amphibian An animal that can breathe in air and water, which includes frogs, toads, newts and salamanders.

brackish A mixture of river water and seawater.

crustacean A group of mainly water animals that includes crabs, lobsters and shrimps.

hyoid bone A U-shaped bone in the neck.

keratin A material that makes up the structure of hair, feathers, hooves, claws and scales.

mollusc A family of animals that includes snails, slugs, mussels and octopuses.

predator An animal that hunts and eats other animals.

prey An animal that is hunted and eaten by another animal.

Index

anole lizard 5

chameleon 8–11
cobra 20
crocodile 12–15

dinosaur 12

eggs 7, 17, 19, 23

fangs 20, 22

Komodo dragon 4

lizard 4–7, 9, 20

poison 20, 22

scales 4, 14, 19, 23, 24
snake 20–23

terrapin 17
tortoise 17
turtle 16–19